TABLE OF CONTENTS:

CHAPTER 1: How to Use This Book (pg. 3)

CHAPTER 2: The Passive Income Business Model (pg. 4)

CHAPTER 3: How to Get an Ivy League Education for FREE (pg. 6)

CHAPTER 4: 20 Companies that Will Pay You to Work from Home (pg. 8)

CHAPTER 5: 40 Ways to Make Money Online *(A step-by-step guide)*

1. Blogging………12
2. **Create a Website: How to Double Traffic**………14

3. Google AdSense………15
4. Affiliate Marketing………16
5. Write an eBook………17
6. Be Artsy on Etsy…………17
7. Selling on eBay vs. Amazon………18
8. Play Games— That's Right!……… 19
9. Become a Virtual Assistant………20
10. Enter Competitions………20
11. College Students: Scholarships………23
12. Create a Fundraiser……….24
13. Sponsored Tweets………. 24
14. Freelance Writing (+Tips)………… 24
15. Get Free Stuff on Craigslist………...28
16. Sell Stock Photos………. 29
17. Test Mobile Apps (uTest)……….29
18. Get Paid to Answer Questions……….30
19. Flip Domain Names…………31
20. Get Paid to Live Aboard (Without ANY Expenses!)……….32
21. Become a Mystery Shopper………33
22. Build a Mobile App (for Non-Techies)………… 34

23.	Refer Your Friends for Jobs............35	
24.	Create YouTube Videos............35	
25.	Design Logos..........36	
26.	Design T-Shirts and Other Items (Hassle-Free)........37	
27.	Create Social Media Graphics: A 14-Year Old Did It!..........38	
28.	Online Surveys and Offers..........39	
29.	Design Websites— Without HTML Knowledge.........41	
30.	Start a Free Online Forum............42	

A List of More Ideas: #31-40.............43

CHAPTER 1: How to Use This Book

What makes this book different from thousands of others is that with this resource, you can jump directly into action. I give you all of the specifics— the best websites to choose and the most certified choices, all from my own experimentations. The research for this book took over an entire year. Every website mentioned and list offered in this book was personally tried out in order to guarantee the best mix.

This book is recommended for the entire family, of all ages. There are many options available in this book that any adult, college graduate, or high school student can pursue, from building websites to creating your own graphic t-shirt line. Even your little kids or students can take advantage of the ample opportunities unrevealed further, including learning how to code, earning money playing games, and a myriad of prestigious competitions that will open many more doors for the future.

I would like to think of Chapters 2-4 as an introductory prelude to the world of online monetization. After learning about the many resources at hand, perhaps you will then become ready to dive in Chapter 5: 40 Ways to Make Money Online.

Chapter 5 is unique. Instead of merely listing off 40 ways, each option is dissected into its exact step-by-step method of action. The beginning for each option may seem daunting. It will be. Hard work is needed to initiate the activity, but after the launch, you will be able to lean back and enjoy a constant, passive income. Soon enough, you will be banking in your sleep!

CHAPTER 2: The Passive Income Business Model

Let's start off with a scenario. Suppose you have a passion for DIY handcrafts and fashion made from old scrap-clothing. So you create a blog updating your friends and family on your latest crafts (the individual steps are outlined in Chapter 5). You later decide that you want to make money off your hobby, capitalizing on your niche that's uniquely defined, yet has plenty of Google searches.

There are numerous options you can now take, or perhaps you wish to take more than one. You can set up advertisements on the sides of your webpage, sell an eBook, create YouTube videos, try out affiliate marketing, or sell your items online. You love writing and teaching others, so you decide to write an eBook and make YouTube videos in the end.

Like I mentioned before, the key to every passive income ending is hard work. Banish every marketing rouse that tried to persuade you that you can earn thousands fast. Like the claim 'Lose weight fast,' the passive income business model requires progressive, hard work in order to reach the ultimate goal.

Now back to our scenario. Using the techniques illustrated in Chapter 5, you use Google AdSense to display a small column of ads on the very side. You've now also written an eBook called "Frugal

Fashion," which is reasonably priced on your website and other online bookstores. Additionally, you update your YouTube channel with many DIY and information videos, working as a YouTube partner and always linking back to your blog page.

So is that it? You've finished most of your main content by now. However, if you stop now, you might be disappointed with the lack of income coming in. Even the best of us wish to avoid this step, but we all need some marketing. You need to get the information out there that your website exists and it's worthy of other people's time. After being spread around, people from New Zealand to Florida check out your blog and share it via word-of-mouth or social media sites.

Finally! You're almost at the finish line. Sometime around now you will take the best sleep of your life and wake up to find your PayPal account numerically higher than it was merely eight hours before, and you were sleeping right through the transaction!

Perhaps two people bought your eBook, a small store in Hong Kong purchased your new line of clothing, or your blog got passed around for even more views. And perhaps with this increase of free time you have, you decide to create another online business detailed later on in this book (so you have extra modes of income).

You might even get to quit that day job and focus on the hobbies that you enjoy the most! And that's what I call the 'Passive Income Business Model.'

CHAPTER 3: How to Get an Ivy League Education for Free

Education has never been more accessible, and without losing its appeal or quality. Many professors around the world from the most prestigious universities have made their lectures, exams, and course notes available online, to simulate the classroom experience as closely as possible.

This mode of learning was first established when two computer science professors from Stanford University created Coursera.org to make courses from engineering to the humanities accessible for anyone from the comforts of their home.

Following in the steps of **Coursera**, numerous other websites sprung up that also offered free services. Here's a list:

- Coursera
- Udacity
- edX
- Stanford Online
- Class2Go
- Venture Lab

Of course, great resources such as **Khan Academy** cannot be left out. There are also websites that contain a lot of good information, but without certification:

- TED Talks
- MIT OpenCourseWare
- IIT Open Courses (NPTEL)
- Open Yale Courses

Learn How to Code.

With this modern era so computer-focused, it's becoming more useful than ever to know how to code. Fortunately, there are also many online resources that are able to break down the information for us to digest. Learn how to build apps, games, program, and HTML with the following:

- Codeacademy
- Treehouse
- Khan Academy

- Google Code University

If you would like to expose your kids or students to coding, try **Hour of Code** on Code.org. For instance, kids can understand the basics of programing with Angry Birds and the help of Mark Zuckerberg and Bill Gates. However, nobody's ever too old (or young) to learn how to code!

CHAPTER 4: 20 Companies that Will Pay You to Work from Home

Ever wanted to make your dreams of living in a tropical distant island real? Okay, perhaps you can also resort to stay within the comfort of your house. But here are 20 real companies that will pay you to work online, so you can be at any location of your preference. You might not have heard of some of these companies on this list, but that's the point— exploring new territory leads to new options that might suit you even better.

1) **About.com**

This content-rich website requests for skilled writers that often specialized in their field of expertise. And they will pay you well for that knowledge as well; many guides have been rumored to take away up to $100,000 a year! (Refer to Chapter 5, #14: Freelance Writing for more details)

2) **Amazon**

Amazon is hiring for their virtual customer service center, as well as openings for the technical support team.

3) **Applied Medical Services**

You can get the job if you have at least two years of experience as a medical transcriptionist. With that, you will receive competitive pay rates, holiday and premium weekend pay.

4) U-haul

With the ability to choose your own work hours, this is a flexible opportunity to earn extra bucks. You will answer calls pertaining to scheduling and general moving questions.

5) GoFluent.com

Are you multilingual? Use your skills to teach others! The company prefers native English speakers fluent in Russian, French, German, Italian, or Japanese.

6) Arise

Working through Arise allows you to work with many major brands. Positions include tech positions, customer service, sales, and Mac owner opportunities.

7) Speak Write

Challenge yourself— so are you able to transcribe (non-medical) information? Take one hour shifts in transcribing audio. Great for college students, and fast typists can earn up to $15 an hour.

8) Brainmass.com

With a graduate degree, you can be a teaching assistant answering student questions. When students purchase credit to have their questions answered, a portion of the credit will be paid to you.

9) WiseBread

Think you're a personal finance expert? Have a knack for blogging? Consider writing for WiseBread.com. Have three sample blog posts prepared for the application process.

10) 1800Flowers.com

Both full-time and part-time employees are sought after for this reputable company. Pay is about $9 an hour, and products include flowers, cakes, chocolate, and gift baskets.

11) Demand Studios

Another freelance writing opportunity, Demand Studios allows you to choose upon a variety of topics to be published on eHow, Livestrong, and other online brands.

12) Clarity Consultants

Get paid for giving away your advice! This company brings together clients and consultants (you) together.

13) Leapforce

Leapforce hires Google Raters to evaluate search engine results. You can choose to work part-time or full-time, and you're also given an hourly, competitive pay.

14) Sylvan Learning

If you have at least a bachelor's degree, you can tutor students online with the subject of your choice.

15) HomeworkTutoring.com

With a webcam and online messaging, you can tutor students with homework help. Current topics include history, law, and engineer— you can also suggest another subject to work with.

16) WeGoLook.com

Do you want to be a "looker?" You can perform tasks either online or off, with a starting pay of $25 or above, depending on the project on hand.

17) Cloud Crowd

A "micro-work" company, Cloud Crowd requires that you download their Facebook app in order to complete projects and tasks for various companies.

18) BalanceYourBooks.com

A great opportunity if you are a CPA or book keeper with a bit of working experience.

19) E-Poll

For an easy way to earn a couple of bucks, E-Poll allows you to take some simple surveys in exchange for gift cards or money into your PayPal account.

20) ITT Technical Institute

If you have a postgraduate degree, you can apply to work as a professor and teach online classes!

CHAPTER 5: 40 Smart Ways to Make Money Online

1. Blogging

You can easily earn a living from blogging if people find your content interesting or valuable enough. As a blogger myself, the first rule to blogging is to make it into something that's enjoyable.

To become a successful blogger, you'll find yourself churning out posts on a routine basis, so it's more than crucial to blog about something that interests *you.*

Setting up a blog can seem difficult at first. Just searching up how-to on Google can overwhelm anyone after reading web terms such as domain name, web-hosting, and WordPress. I'll process and break the information down for you.

Blogger.

This is Google's blog publishing tool that's 100% free and easy to use. The only catch is that you won't be able to possess your own domain name. That's the word 'domain name' again!

Allow me to first explain what that is. A domain name is your website's address. For example: *domain-name-here.com.*

But with blogger, instead of domainname.com, you have domainname.blogspot.com. It's a small difference, but that can be the difference between looking professional or not, and having your viewers remember your blog when they wish to revisit.

The good thing about Blogger is that your blog will be search-optimized. That means Google will put your blog farther above other searches, since Google is always trying to highlight its own services. Plus, you can create a blog in less than a minute—no joke!

Getting Your Own Domain Name.

This pathway may seem the most ideal for most bloggers, and a component that most popular blogs share: an individualized domain name. This choice can take a little bit longer in the beginning, but soon enough your website can launch off ahead of all other searches. Let me guide you through with the following steps:

1) Register a Domain Name.
Go to a reputable domain name registrar such as GoDaddy, Network Solutions, or Publish247. Many

of these sites may also offer you free domain names if you buy a package that includes web hosting. That takes us to the next step.

2) Choose a Web Host.

In layman terms, hosting a website makes it accessible on the World Wide Web. Therefore, you can't skip this step. Determine the best place to host your website depending on your personal finances and how popular your blog might be.

Remember, you pay roughly for what you use. For instance, if you're expecting thousands of visitors a day, stay away from cheaper "starter" packages, unless you can deal with your website constantly crashing.

3) WordPress.

Since you are blogging, the best and most notable blogging platform is WordPress. (Or you can build up a HTML website from scratch… but I won't get into that.) You won't need to know how to code, so being non-technical is no problem. WordPress has some standard free templates for your website. If you're not satisfied with the look, you can purchase other templates or find another site that offers templates, such as WooThemes.

Whew—that was a lot! I'll first add pointers in #2: "Create a Website", but for the points that follow, you will find how to **monetize your blog or website.**

2. Create a Website: How to Double Traffic

The steps to create a website are the same as those of a blog: registering domain name, web hosting, and WordPress. But there are a few other bits that can boost your number of visitors and polish your website for optimum results.

Namely, I will list out ways to double your traffic. I have personally tested out all of these points on my own website and doubled my traffic in only 2 months.

Some of you might be frustrated at this point, eager to jump into making money. But that will only set you up for failure. **Monetizing your website can only occur when you actually have visitors.**

Find a Niche.

At this point I'm assuming you are building a content website. If not, feel free to skip ahead.

A niche is any topic or area that people are interested in. This includes hobbies, fitness, food, money, and products. Do keywords research beforehand, as you want to create content that others will actually want to find. Conveniently, Google has a keyword tool.

Your ultimate goal is to create a site that circles around a narrow topic, yet can be broadened out as you wish. Your visitors will hopefully be continuous members, so by focusing on a certain niche, you will be viewed as the expert.

A niche will also be easier to sell certain products that might pertain to visitors, but that will covered later.

Make Use of WordPress Plugins.

The "SiteMap" plugin is important because it generates and submits your blog's sitemap (a listing of all your posts) to all the major engines once installed, therefore increasing traffic.

The "Related Posts" plugin encourages people to read other parts of your blog. This links together your website so that older posts are also visited.

Visual Appeal.

Although this might not directly increase traffic, it does make people more likely to remember your site or stay longer. Be sure to break text with graphics for easy readability. Visiting your website shouldn't be a task but worthy of readers' time.

Post Consistently and Often.

This is a no-brainer, as when you post often, the search engine spiders will visit more frequently. In addition, you won't be unsubscribed from and people will come back frequently for new information.

Now Let's Talk About the Money!

A website is a portal to endless ways to make money online, which is what this book is all about!

3. Google AdSense

Arguably one of the easiest ways to monetize, Google AdSense allows you to choose the size and presentation of advertisements. The revenue earned is a direct relationship to the amount of traffic. Or in other words, more people, more money. Google will only enable this feature if you have a decent amount of content on your website.

With the easy accessibility though, AdSense is best used if you have large amounts of traffic. Logistically speaking, the probability of someone clicking on an ad is 1-2%.

Although Google doesn't publish their policies, you generally get 20 cents per click. For example, if you get 1000 visitors at your website than you will be able to earn anywhere from $2 to $10 each day—definitely not enough for a living.

4. Affiliate Marketing

This is a revenue-sharing plan that gains you commission when the customer clicks on the advertisement. You get money when the customer purchases a product from the advertiser, subscribes to a newsletter, or downloads a link.

You may be paid either pay-per-click (every time someone clicks on the ad), or through a commission rate (usually 10-15%, "pay-per-sale").

Unlike Google AdSense, with affiliate marketing you have complete control over the type of ads displayed. That being said, choose an affiliate program that is marketing a product that you're confident in promoting and relevant to your site.

Which one is better?

Generally speaking, pay-per-click offers the lowest value for conversions (need more clicks), but pay-per-sale programs give you a higher commission (requires less clicks but more unique visitors).

Although I believe pay-per-sale would be better for the long run, use your own traffic and reporting tools to determine which type of program would have a better chance of success on your own site.

5. Write an eBook

The obvious reason why people write ebooks is to sell them for profit on various different places, often allowing you to list your book for free. In case you're interested, here's a comprehensive list:

- Amazon Kindle
- Barnes & Noble
- Clickbank
- Ebay
- Google Books
- PayDotCom
- Smashwords
- Craigslist
- Lulu
- Your Own Website

But unknown to many bloggers, ebooks can maximize your subscribers, increase your revenue (selling from your own website), and boost your credentials.

Many bloggers utilize the method of gaining subscribers this way: requiring visitors to enter their email address to obtain a free eBook. This keeps allows you to keep them updated on new posts or something that entices them to constantly revisit your website, like freebies and contests. So even if you offer your eBook for free, there are tons of options available for you!

If creating a website isn't in your best interests, then there are still plenty of options available for you! Continue to read on.

6. Be Artsy on Etsy

Etsy.com is an e-commerce website that enables art lovers to sell art supplies, photos, and handmade or vintage items. The cost is reasonably low, about $0.20 per listing for 3 months, and available for 5 images.

Any Tips?

Since Etsy is so popular, the competition can be fierce for most areas. To leverage the most out of your products, use all of your keywords and think like a buyer.

Another tip is spend time on Etsy's community forums. Offer quality information and answer questions; you never know when you could be talking to a potential buyer.

7. Selling on eBay vs. Amazon

So where does the difference exist? Here are a few takes:

Amazon.

You will attract more buyers by selling items that are in brand new or "like new" condition. So if you're items aren't that used, then Amazon would be a better bet.

One of their nice features is that you don't have to pay a listing fee if your item doesn't sell. Once sold, Amazon earns their cut based on their set percentages for the type of item (ranging from 6-15%).

eBay.

Unlike Amazon, eBay requires you to upload a picture and provide a brief description. If you need quick money, eBay would be the better option. Amazon usually has a two-week hold on your money, so if you need the money fast, go eBay.

Essentially, the marketplace potential rests on the individual product you're trying to sell and your personal preferences. Do some prior research to view your competition and determine from there whether or not the listing will benefit you.

8. Play Games—That's Right!

Nope, you didn't just misread that. There are a few online websites that allow you to earn online money and then later convert it into money rewards. It's an easy way to accumulate points when you can play some games during breaks or downtime.

Swagbucks.

'Swag' may seem like a hackneyed word used by some delusional teenagers, but we could make an exception for this site. You can earn 'swagbucks' rather easily by playing online games, answering their daily polls, and using their own search engine instead of Google's.

After a certain amount, you can convert it into gift cards to any popular store: Amazon, Target, Barnes and Nobles, or even to your PayPal account.

Instant Cash Sweepstakes.

There is no need to spend more than 5 minutes a day taking their quick survey games. Most of the questions don't even have wrong answers. If you answer the few quick surveys, you can win a few cents, enter in the daily sweepstakes of

$50, and earn "coins" to spend in a separate $2 drawing that happens every few hours which you can cash out for $2 at PayPal.

I've personally won the $2 and $50 drawing a couple of times, which certainly adds up. Not bad for something I spend less than 5 minutes a day doing.

Game Show Network.

They offer arcade games, trivia games, and game shows that are played in conjunction to those shown on their network. You earn Oodles, the online currency, which you can later trade in for gift cards and cash prizes.

Tip: Increase your daily earnings by using the Swagbucks search engine (see above) to look up trivia questions!

9. Become a Virtual Assistant

A virtual assistant is someone that provides administrative support or other specialized services to other individuals or small businesses. Depending on your client, they might require you to set up their schedule, answer emails, manage their blog, or even to just remind them about due dates.

Advertise your special skills on contracting sites such as Elance, ODesk, and Guru. To make yourself even more marketable, it helps to get a certification that establishes your expertise and join an acknowledged organization, like the International Virtual Assistants Association.

10. Enter Competitions

There are a myriad of competitions you can enter, differing from size to subject. Having kept tabs on a range of them myself, I'll divide them into categories and also specify a few that are specifically for high school students as well (great scholarship money— #11: Scholarships also talks about some other options).

***Note:** Contests labeled **'HS' (High School)** are only available for high school students. Even if you're an adult, many of the contests are a good opportunity for your child or even your neighbor's child.

Art Contests.

- **Doodle 4 Google, grades 3-12**— Google is rich, so their contests are both competitive and munificent. The national winner earns $30,000 for college, $50,000 for their school's computer lab, a trip to NYC, and their "doodle" published on Google's front page. Not bad! The national finalists from each state also earn rewards along the way.

- **Scholastic Art and Writing Awards, HS**— Considered the most prestigious art and writing competition for high school students, Scholastic Awards can be entered for poetry, photography, art, video games, and fashion. The Alliance offers over $250,000 in scholarships to their top winners.

- **AllArtCompetitions.com**— This website provides an extensive range of art contests that usually don't require a fee from you. They display contests that will award you anywhere from $500 to $20,000+ in cash prizes.

Writing Contests.

- **Writer's Digest**— The magazine holds annual contests on every writing genre. They offer thousands of dollars in rewards, but the best part of it is having published magazine work and the recognition for aspiring writers.

- **AynRandNovels.org, HS Essay Contests**— The Ayn Rand Foundation is extremely generous with providing scholarships. For instance, the essays for "The Fountainhead" and "Atlas Shrugged" both provide $10,000 for the 1st prize winner, as well as money down to the 175 semifinalists.

- **Poets & Writers (pw.org/grants)**— P&W has a large database filled with writing competitions.

Their list is more than comprehensive and published in their magazine annually.

- **Magazines, Stores, and More**— Check in year-round for your favorite magazines. Chances are that they will probably be hosting a number of contests that offer cash, sweepstakes, or tropical getaways. Some magazine ideas may include O Magazine, Taste of Home, or Glamour.
Additionally, you can look up giveaways from Food Network, Ellen, and contests hosted by a few retail stores.

Photography Contests.

- **Photo Contest Insider**— Their website displays a host of photography contests to be checked out.

- **Sony World Photography Awards**— Calling all passionate photographers, the Sony World Awards will offer you one stellar prize: the L'Iris d'Or and $25,000.

Science and Tech Contests.

- **Google Science Fair, HS**— Kids are changing the world, and this international contest is just proof. With prizes along the way, the grand winner will receive a $50,000 scholarship and a free foreign adventure that's different each year. Not to mention that every college will love you.

- **Siemens Competition, HS**— The Siemens Foundation partnered up with College Board to offer a nationally recognized math, science, and technology competition. Winning projects range from $1,000 to $100,000.

- **The DuPont Challenge, Science Essay, grades 7-12**— DuPont gives all of their winners U.S. Savings Bonds and prizes that total up to $100,000. There are a total of 4 essay categories for both the middle and high school divisions.

Speech Contests.

- **Voice of Democracy, HS**— The Veteran of Foreign Wars (VFW) hosts this audio speech contest for high school students (they also have Patriot's Pen, an essay contest for middle school students). The national winner earns a whopping $30,000 and other winners can earn money at each level.

- **American Legion Oratorical Competition, HS**— The title is a handful, and so may the contest requirements itself. Competitors present an 8-10 minute on a prepared speech on some aspect of the U.S. Constitution, and a 3-5 minute speech on an assigned topic (over 1 of the 4 amendments). But in return, students are rewarded in scholarships at the local, state, and national levels. The national winner also receives an $18,000 scholarship.

That being said, even if the contests above don't apply to your interests, you are bound to find a competition that matches your skills.

11. College Students: Scholarships

There are two valuable resources every student should know about: **Scholarships.com** and **Zinch.com**. Besides posting their own scholarship opportunities, both websites also display tons of others.

I have tried every website listed in this book and dozens of others that I choose to leave out due to lack of user-friendliness or other difficulties. And personally, I find Zinch to be less of a hackle, especially for frustrated parents and students overwhelmed with the college application process (fewer advertisements, easier layout, and more scholarships).

But at the same time, money is money, and for whatever Zinch leaves out, Scholarships fills in.

12. Create a Fundraiser

This is another option to fund your way through school, or anything from medical procedures to new business ventures. There are many sites for this specific purpose, such as GoEnnounce, but you can also create your own site to set up your fundraiser.

Unless your case is extremely compelling or you are in dire need, most strangers won't help you out. But that's why we have our family and friends right? Basically, these websites give you the option to ask around for funding without having to ask face to face.

The best way to promote your fundraiser is to send out a link to all of your relatives and posting it on all of your social media networks explaining your need. Good luck!

13. Sponsored Tweets

SponsoredTweets.com is a website platform that connects tweeters to advertisers that wish to pay for their social media presence. If you have a bunch of followers, you can sign up today to start earning money.

14. Freelance Writing (+Tips)

There are many websites and online magazines that will pay for your articles. Your income reflects the popularity of your pages, so reader loyalty and SEO wording are both crucial. Also keep in mind the places that allow you to republish articles and the others that require exclusive articles.

If you don't have any prior experience freelancing, there will be fewer places that will accept your work and you can't expect constant writing assignments at first. Nevertheless, every successful freelancer started off in this position.

Let's start analyzing the many options available; I will outline employers from low to high acceptability in publishing your work.

Freelance Writing Websites— a list of ideas. . .

- ELance
- Helium
- oDesk
- Freelancer
- Squidoo
- Constant-Content
- Craigslist
- ArticleMe

Yahoo! Voices

After signing into Yahoo! Contributor Network, you have the choice to write from their Assignment Desk or any article of your own preference. And as long as you follow their basic guidelines, Yahoo! will publish basically anything. But at the same time, their pay is rather low.

Tip: Filling out your public profile and uploading a professional avatar picture can help you tremendously in sending assignments along your way. Also, publish more content to gain readership and to be featured more prominently.

Check out some additional tips on how to boost your article views and search engine listings at the end of #14: "Freelance Writing".

eHow.com

The source for how-to articles was recently purchased by Demand Media Studios, which is where your application should be sent to. The company also owns other websites like LIVESTRONG.com, USAToday.com, as well as others.

It could be a great start to earn small money, but that's it. Once you become familiar with their guidelines, it's easier to produce content fast. Find a good number that you're comfortable with and set a goal. For instance, at 5 articles a day, and you can easily make some side income and, at the same time, profit from some of your older posts.

About.com

One of the top information sites, About.com searches for professionals for their specialized topics. Even so, there may be only a few topics available for grabs. You can choose to be a contributing writer, 12 articles a month for $500/month guaranteed for the first year; or you might even be able to be a topic guide.

If you become accepted as a topic guide, you have the potential to make a decent living off of the job. As a recognized expert in your field, the average guide earns $24,000/year, but many guides have earned anywhere from $72,000 to $100,000 a year, depending on personal performance.

HowStuffWorks.com

HowStuffWorks is very selective and has the power to be as choosy as they want. Owned and operated by Discovery Communications, the website favors professors and specialists over general freelancers. Although they don't publicly post their compensation rates, it is a known fact among the freelancing community that you can expect $100-$300 for an article.

Now, let's move onto freelancing tips that will improve your search listings and augment your chances for the job.

Tips: Steps to Increase Your Income

1. **List keywords and key phrases**— This isn't written in your article, but your publisher usually will ask you to include this for the page's meta-data. WikiHow provides a sound explanation:

    "Key phrases and keywords are registered by so-called "spiders," which are scripts that search engines send out to every page on the

Internet. These spiders "crawl" across web pages and websites and analyze them for content and <u>quality of content</u>. One of the ways they do this is to register the keywords and key phrases to determine the subject of a page; but they also detect <u>how often each key word or phrase is used</u>."

2. **Create hyperlinks**— These are the links inserted within the article that navigate the reader to other relevant content. Use hyperlinks to your advantage; navigate the reader to pertinent articles written by you.

3. **Write titles that win**— Web users are faced with dozens of similar options when they search for information on the web. But how can you come out in the head of the gang? And that's why titles are everything. I've found a repeated cycle online from the top posts of the most successful content writers. Here is a hypothetical 'Top 5 Posts' list:

- "How to Eliminate Procrastination for Good"

- "23 Secret Foods to Boost Your Metabolism"
- "Badass Frugal Tips: What You're Doing Wrong"
- "Why Your Desk is Killing You"
- "Top 10 Reasons Why You're Still Single"

Have you seen the pattern yet? The titles that people actually click on show a common problem and give an alternative implementation, use the term "How To", or contain numerical lists. So write titles that are engaging and ensure the reader that they won't be wasting their time by clicking!

In Conclusion: The points above are all SEO tips. 'SEO' sounds like an awfully fancy word, especially for beginners wishing to start freelancing, but it just stands for "Search Engine Optimization"— or how you can put your content at the top of any search engine.

Whether you want to build a website, freelance, or create an app, you will face some technical explanations all over the web that might turn you off. (But don't give up!) If you need, just remember to break it down. Keep everything plain and simple.

15. Get Free Stuff on Craigslist

Too many people overlook the opportunities on Craigslist, but the truth is that if you know where to look, you can dig up a gold mine. I've found free puppies, furniture, scrap metal, and trees.

To get stuff on Craigslist for free, search on your local Craigslist page. Click on a section called "Free" under the "For Sale" category. You will immediately find a list of postings from the most recent date. Now all you need to do is call up the owner and pick up the item.

Craigslist Cleaning Business.

You can keep the item, or you can make some money off of it. Spend a few minutes to clean it up. If possible, try to make the item look as nice as you can. For instance, if you have a desk, apply a new coat of paint or polish to it.

From there, you could resell it on Craigslist, eBay, or Amazon (#7: Selling on eBay vs. Amazon). Make sure to post pictures from different angles and write an attractive posting to convince your buyers.

16. Sell Stock Photos

What's better than to make money while pursuing your hobby? Many magazines, writers, and designers are buying stock photos instead of paying the expense for a professional photographer.

You could be an amateur and still sell with success. Just make sure your photos are crisp and clear; a little editing doesn't hurt. Some places to upload on include iStockphoto, Fotolia, and ShutterStock.

Choose the correct category so clients can find you easily and add several tags. With a collection of photographs online, you could be earning a nice side income.

17. Test Mobile Apps (uTest)

There are many platforms available for users to test new apps. I'm going to divide this part into 2 sections: for professional software testers and everybody else.

User Testing.

Website owners find testers from UserTesting.com to examine the website's clarity and usability. If you decide to become a tester, all you then need is User Testing's screen-capturing software, a computer microphone, and a few minutes of quiet time for each site.

The Wall Street Journal commented on the site design: "Website testers make about $10 for spending 15 to 25 minutes trying out sites and recording their opinions." Good Morning America also reviewed it, saying that you're paid $10 for doing 10-20 minutes of work.

Just keep in mind that they might limit the number of users that sign up, and assignments are on a first come, first serve basis, and offers get claimed fairly quickly. Expect 10 completed tests ($100) on a decent month.

uTest.

A software and mobile app testing company, uTest requires you to have experience in software programming or the likes. You can apply for testing in either one of the following areas: functional, load, security, usability, and localization.

Remember, I'm just contributing suggestions for places to look, most of which are the most popular options at the point of this book. To find the right fit for you, be sure to compare with other sites as well.

18. Get Paid to Answer Questions

Many websites pay you for answering questions and giving advice. Submit your application to a website you'll trust under the area of your knowledge.

Your best bet would be to join multiple websites so you can increase your earning potential. Nevertheless, every website has its own benefits, so I've listed some for you to determine for yourself.

- **Knowbrainers**— Customer payment for general knowledge, pop culture, and sports questions are usually $3-$10. Pet questions are $10-$25, and health is $25-$60.

- **ChaCha**— Become a ChaCha guide to answer questions. Since the service is based off of customers who are using their mobile phones, expect questions like: "How can I find the nearest and cheapest gas station from here?" Other questions include stocks, travel, entertainment, and places.

- **StudentQuestions**— Provide homework help with thorough answers. If a student chooses your answer, he or she will then pay you through PayPal with a small rate going as commission. Another similar site is **AceYourCollegeClasses.com**.

- **Yahoo! Answers**— Although they don't actually pay for your answers, this is the most popular Q&A site. That means it's a great place where you can recommend products for your affiliate sales or recommend searchers to visit your website. Just be sure not to spam and try to provide useful information.

- **WpQuestions**— All WordPress experts, you can now earn anywhere from $5-$100 for your knowledge per question. (If you look back at #1: Blogging, you can read more about WordPress). And if you have a blog filled with content, you can also consider **Askables.com**—where you get paid for the amount of work you get done instead of traffic.

19. Flip Domain Names

Flipping domain names is essentially buying and selling virtual real estate. Many people earn thousands after they purchase the right domain names. Forbes recently published a story about a high school senior, Steven McDonald, who grossed $325,000 in a year from doing so.

Domain names can be extremely cheap; on some sites, you can buy one for as little as $7 a year. But to make the big profit, you have to snatch up the names with the biggest potential. Most four-letter names have already been taken back in the 90's, such as fund.com which sold for $10 million.

What are in the market right now are short domain names or acronyms. A great example is cpc.com. Sold for

$202,000 to Contract Pharmacal Corp., it was the highest reported sale for a three-letter domain. That just goes to show that short, seemingly random acronyms might luckily lead you to traders or corporations that will offer a high price.

Another option is to follow what people are generally searching for. Check out the Google Adwords keyword tool (adwords.google.com) for the most popular searches.

Generally, there is a hierarchy to the rankings of domain names. Shorter is better and a name ending with ".com" is more valuable. Moving fast will also aid you—snatch up the domain names of novel companies before they realize what they need. You can usually sell domain names on certain auction sites when you are ready to monetize.

20. Get Paid to Live Aboard (Without ANY Expenses!)

Living aboard has vast benefits. It's also cheaper to live in developing countries (as opposed to developed countries and third-world nations), especially when you're comparing the cost of living with that of the US, Canada, Australia, and the UK.

You can enjoy your exotic existence when you have some passive income revenue— say, from working online. But at the same time, you might want to opt for something that's more financially friendly, or the expense-free version.

Listed below are options where you don't have to pay a dime for even room or board.

Teach English in Asia.

To clear things up, you can teach English (or any other subject) wherever you would like; however, many nations in Asia have a huge demand for fluent English-speaking teachers. When looking for a market, you would want a place that demands such a need and is economically robust. For example, many international schools and universities in China will eagerly accept English teachers and pay for all of their expenses plus a regular paycheck.

You don't have to be fluent in the new language, but just eager to learn. Make sure you have the qualifications to teach; schools that don't require so usually will hire anyone, pay very little, and provide little to no academic support.

On the other hand, to get qualified for high-paying jobs at universities, international schools, or in the government, you almost always are required to hold a master's degree in a relevant subject. This is true especially in Asian countries where qualifications are everything.

Work on an Organic Farm.

Many unemployed college graduates choose this pathway instead of trying to struggle off of a menial to nonexistent income. And for the avid green thumb travelers, this experience is a way to see the lands and live a life beyond the usual scope of our daily lives.

You may work a few hours a day on a participating farm in exchange for home-cooked food and accommodation. World Wide Opportunities on Organic Farms is one place to look, although they don't pay for travel costs.

Other Ideas.

From every line of work, you can get paid to go international. Work on cruise ships, where you can have fun while earning a fantastic paycheck. Travel blog about your experiences. Start an adventure travel company. Take your consulting job global and meet your international clients.

Do all of the above opportunities sound risky, out of your comfort zone? Well they should be. It's your choice whether to remain static or land the job of your dreams.

21. Become a Mystery Shopper

Mystery shoppers, or secret shoppers, pose as regular customers to evaluate the quality of goods and services that the business provides. You would then give a detailed report to the mystery shopping company so that they could report the findings back to the business.

Many businesses including groceries, theatres, retail stores, restaurants, resorts, and hotels use mystery shoppers. You might have to take some pictures or record conversations with employees to administer a better report.

Check out Volition.com for a database of reputable mystery shopping companies to start out with. Send an application to a list of companies you're interested in working for. They usually pay $10-15 for each shop; you will also get paid back for any purchases you had to make.

Before you consent to an offer, make sure you are being compensated for your time. For example, $25 might sound like a good deal until you realize that you will be spending 5 hours in that single shop.

If you don't want to leave the comfort of your home, there are also plenty of mystery shoppers online-hunting for virtual businesses. When you're starting out though, you might have to front the costs of your purchases to prove your capability first.

Unfortunately, there are also mystery shopping companies posing as scams. Avoid anyplace that requires you to pay to earn assignments or a shopper certification; you shouldn't have to pay anything.

22. Build a Mobile App (for Non-Techies)

Paradoxically, we have to thank technology for the ability to create technology without any of the knowledge. For all of us non-techies, we no longer need to know how to code to create an app!

Of course you can't design beautiful games or apps that require teams of programmers, but some of us don't need that and desire web apps instead.

There are an abundance of websites that allow you to convert your website, blog, or Facebook into something that you can sell on iTunes or Google Play.

Everyone will obviously like a different app creator, so I've included a few of the popular converters that I've also personally used:

- Conduit (mobile.conduit.com)
- AppsBar
- Buzztouch
- And literally hundreds others!

Let's start with a pragmatic scenario. You are a musician hoping to share an app so that your followers can find your updates at easily. Using an app creator website, you insert the links that you'd like to include: your Twitter feed, music from your Facebook group, uploaded songs on Sound Cloud, and your website.

Immediately, all of your content is synchronized onto the app simulator on the right side of the screen, so you will be able to view it from a user's perspective. Fix or add other feeds and as simple as that, you're ready to upload your new app in the marketplace!

23. Refer Your Friends for Jobs

Be able to get your friends hired to a new job and earn some money along the way. It's a win-win situation: the outcome that I like the best. If you can stand behind their work ethic and skills, consider helping them gain the attention of prospective employers. And remember to ask them to take you out for a free drink following their new employment, eh?

Websites like ReferEarns, WhoDoYouKnowForDough, and Refer.ly are all places where you can refer other skilled professionals. And if they get hired, as the middleman, you can get anywhere from fifty to a few thousand dollars depending on the position.

24. Create YouTube Videos

The new policy created in 2011 allowed anyone to become a YouTube partner. That means that you can even monetize if you have a single video. Although you would probably only be earning a few bucks for every 1,000 views, if you are popular, you can earn up to $100+.

There are a handful of YouTube stars that are able to earn a six-figure salary through their videos. Popular areas include beauty and makeup, entertainment, and tutorials. Many makeup gurus increase their income through product sponsorships. Companies send in their products for free so that the YouTuber would give it a mention.

YouTube videos can be highly functional in other areas too. If you own a website, embed a YouTube video with a short introduction above it and, optionally, a transcript below for those who would rather read.

Since Google is striving to create a balance between videos and written web content through their listings, a video can increase your traffic.

Bonus: video views from your website also count as views on YouTube!

25. Design Logos

If you have a bit of designing sense, you can easily find a job. There are hundreds of new companies and websites popping up every day, and they all need a label of representation. You can quickly build a business off of logo designing. Post offers on webmaster-related forums and classified ad sites.

Perhaps you have the professional tool, but perhaps you don't and wish to opt out on expensive software. In that case, you can use PhotoFilter for free to create your images.

So what makes a great logo? Nike's visual representation quickly comes into mind. The most important rule to this is to keep it simple. Don't try to create something complicated or trendy; it might be in fashion now, but like all things trendy, it will become outdated. You want something classic and timeless with a limited color palette.

Another rule to keep in mind is to utilize the usage of the logo. Remember that logos are there to create a brand that people will remember and easily recognize. Although it seems like common sense, many people forget to create a logo that reflects the company's "vision" and can endure versatility.

26. Design T-shirts and Other Items (Hassle-Free)

You can now sell your t-shirt designs without having to deal with manufacturing, customer service, payments, or stocking products. There are a few websites that can do it for you. And you aren't limited; slap on your designs on t-shirts, coffee mugs, posters, and more customable items.

Not artistic? That's fine. In fact, some of the best-selling designs display catchy phrases or simple drawings with funny sayings. To create more complex graphic images, the professionals all use Illustrator and Photoshop. Check out WeGraphics.net, a great website filled with useful tutorials for designers and beginners alike.

I'll analyze some t-shirt designing companies in terms of quality, designer commission fee, and other important criteria.

Avoid: CaféPress.

This was one of the most popular options, amassing a large community of dedicated designers. Unfortunately, like many companies when getting big, it started to slash the fees given to designers until they would barely be able to receive any profit.

The most common complaint seems to be quality. It's important for t-shirts to be printed using certain techniques for high-quality control instead of low grade printing that would quickly fade away.

RedBubble.

If you're an artist, it is likely that you have found many cheap designs to be tasteless and disdainful. RedBubble is a growing company with a community of real artists and inspiring designs. They use digital printing with pretty good quality and print on demand.

SpreadShirt.

They use the plot method print (Vector/Flock/Flex), one of the best quality that you will find. Their base prices are cheaper; however, their marketplace is less than orderly. In order to climb up the listings, you must be able to sell more than those who are already at top.

Yerzies uses the plot printing technique too. You can try this company out, as many designers recommend it if you are creating your first shop.

Zazzle.

Optimize your shop for the search engines, and you will have a higher chance of being found. One of the best for digital prints and it also prints on demand.

27. Create Social Media Graphics: A 14-Year Old Did It!

I have always found stories of teenagers who became self-made millionaires to be inspiring. It is just the voice within our head that reminds us that such possibilities are certainly achievable. Let's analyze one particular case example.

Back in 2004 and just 14-years old, Ashley Qualls created Whateverlife.com as a personal portfolio of graphics and pictures. She offered free MySpace layouts and HTML tutorials for other teenagers. The website was supported entirely by advertisement revenue which added up to over $1 million.

The same opportunities are available now. With social media continually posing as a domineering factor of young adult's lives, this area provides tons of creativity and potential. Create Twitter backgrounds, Facebook graphics, or even MySpace layouts and choose whether you wish to distribute them for free or a small price.

28. Online Surveys and Offers

I personally don't like this method as I find it time-consuming and mind numbing. However, some people like the idea of earning easy cash without having to do any real work other than filling out surveys and offers.

You definitely won't get rich from doing surveys; perhaps a few cents or dollars, but it could be a great thing to do during TV commercials or other downtime periods. Payments are usually through PayPal or check, although very few accept users outside Canada, US, UK, and Australia. Some sites that are recommended by surveyors include:

- **Opinion Outpost**— Give your thoughts to receive cash and prizes.

- **Survey Spot**— One of the top panels that pays cash and sends multiple offers daily. You can also request a check if you earn over $5.

- **Survey Savvy**— A lot of people prefer this company, since it doesn't matter if you, your referrals, or your referrals' referrals complete surveys— you get the pay too.

- **NPD**— This global market research company has provided data to many Fortune 500 companies since 1967. Earn cash and prizes for surveys and referrals.

Watch out for scams that require you to pay to join. Also, if you choose to join other market research companies, be sure to check their reviews beforehand to see if they would actually pay or how much they pay.

Kids: Swagbucks or Other Survey Sites?

For the kids and teens that have tried out surveys and offers, they probably came across sites such as Swagbucks, Points2Shop, or someplace else. I'll try to give my viewpoint on each site after personally trying each one.

Points2Shop.

I tried Points2Shop for three weeks. It's enticing for kids to start out with 250 points ($2.50) in their account upon signing up. However, I've had personal problems with ordering; but perhaps it was a rare incidence. After attempting to purchase an Amazon gift card, my account froze and management dodged my inquiries.

Nevertheless, some people (mostly young teenagers), find the website to be equally appealing as I find it repulsive.

Swagbucks.

I've mentioned Swagbucks in **#8: Play Games— That's Right!** Yes, you can earn points for online games as well as surveys and offers, but I wouldn't try to spend the hours if it's just not your cup of tea. Instead, enter the Swagbucks search engine.

Out of all of the survey sites perused, Swagbucks is the only one that provides a search engine (powered by Ask.com and Google) to earn additional points.

My advice would be to download the toolbar for convenience. Where you can, replace YouTube, Google, and Google Images with Swagbucks. Earn around 20 "Swagpoints" a day ($0.20) just from searching, something that students do a lot. Passively and without the extra effort, you can then switch out 450 points for a $5 gift card.

Other Survey Sites for Kids.

Once a survey site becomes popular, the website commonly opts to reward fewer points to receive the larger amount of sponsorship and advertising money. Do some prior research to find a website that doesn't suck out too much time and provides a good compensation for your efforts.

29. Design Websites— Without HTML Knowledge

So you don't have any experience with website building or designing? Or you only have the faintest idea of what HTML is? No problem. Again, just like #22: Build a Mobile App (for Non-Techies), we can use technology to make technology without having to be a pro.

There are free software up to download that enables you to build nice looking websites fairly easily. Take KompoZer for instance. Although it may not be as stable or possesses fewer features than Adobe Dreamweaver, the fact that it won't cost you a dime is enough for the majority of us.

On the other hand, if you're a serious web designer, Adobe Dreamweaver has always been the golden standard. Most users justify the cost with the all of the bells and whistles that is featured along with the software. Among so is the code hinting and insert menus that let you pull up complex bits of code with just a few easy clicks.

Regardless of which method you choose and price that you find worthy, you must find buyers first. Look for expansive online communities, such as webmaster forums like DigitalPoints and WarriorForum.

30. Start a Free Online Forum

It's in our nature to be social, so it is no surprise that online forums are some of the most visited websites. Online communities are visited often by users who post questions and come back to get answers, as well as people who search around to answer those questions. For every entrepreneur, such a large traffic source translates into high revenue.

But it is not all easy. Especially when starting out, be prepared to invest a lot of time monitoring and replying to discussions. Some forum creators even create multiple avatars to convince newcomers that there's already a large community existing.

Take for instance, College Confidential, a forum for high school students preparing for college. The founders were a senior admissions officer and a college dean. To get started, they wrote a plethora of articles trying to demystify the college admissions process. Although they had to manage the content frequently in the beginning, now the site is mostly autonomous with banner ads and a go-to site for many students.

Below are the steps to create a FREE online forum. You can choose the paid version of course; just register a domain name and web hosting.

1. **Pick a message board application**- Some of the most popular choices include pHpBB, Vanilla, SEO-Boards, and the WordPress forum software, bbPress.

2. **Choose a free hosting service**- There are many sites like Forumotion and Network54 that guide you through the creation process and provide free forum-hosting services.

3. **Set up**- You will need to decide on the basics: avatar size, BBCoding, image hosting, etc. If you feel overwhelmed, keep in mind that the hosting service provides tutorials for guidance.

4. **Marketing**- Spread your link by going to similar forums and blogs. Answer their questions or provide a useful perspective to the discussion, while linking back to your forum.

5. **Managing the community**- Regulate your message boards for disrupting spammers that take away from

the experience. If you don't have the time, you can appoint moderators. Every application also has built-in moderator controls for you to activate.

A List of More Ideas... (#31-40)

This list focuses on additional ideas to explore, either to expand your options or to serve as extra motivation.

31. Freelance Design
32. Transcribe Audio
33. Flip Cars and Houses
34. Sell Your Video Game Accounts
35. Do Data Entry
36. Get FREE Stuff by Rebate
37. File-Sharing
38. Do Webinar Marketing
39. Tutor Online
40. Get Paid to Review

A LETTER FROM THE AUTHOR:

Dear Reader,

I wish you the best of luck when reaching your 'Passive Income Success!' Utilize the methods and techniques as shown in this book and allow your money to continuously grow, even while you're asleep. Coupled with hard work, a necessity before everything else, you can watch your businesses expand exponentially. How exciting! Congratulations on reaching the end of the book— now take action!

Best Wishes,
Lucille Tang

www.ingramcontent.com/pod-product-compliance
Lightning Source LLC
Chambersburg PA
CBHW071755170526
45167CB00003B/1041